The Atmospheric Southern

Roderick Hoyle

ISBN　　(10)　0 –9554110-5-X
　　　　　(13) 978-0-9554110-5-2

First published in 2007 by Kevin Robertson
under the **NOODLE BOOKS** imprint
PO Box 279
Corhampton
SOUTHAMPTON
SO32 3ZX

www.kevinrobertsonbooks.co.uk

Printed in England
By Latimer Trend
Plymouth

Rear cover Winchester City 1965. There was talk at this time of brake vans being abolished - never mind oil lamps, and this van was only ten years old.

Previous page Bramley & Wonersh, Surrey; 1965. I would have preferred some steam machinery in the background, but this view of a keen trainspotter has enough merit: note how he respects the privilege of the opportunity to open wide a window, peer forth if so inclined, whilst enjoying the rush of summer air. Contrast with the mollycoddled attitude of the modern train providers....

(Note - All photographs are by the Author.)

The Atmospheric Southern

Introduction

These images pictures, impressions or whatever they mean to the reader have, during the process of selection, printing and captioning given me a growing sense of shock. I assumed I was - as now - responding visually to my surroundings in an essentially similar way. Maybe so: but the profound difference in the world of rail travel through these decades is very marked, and reflects changes in the world in general.

This introduction however, serves to discuss the motivation in capturing these images [to those who are interested read on: otherwise on with the pictures!]

The period in question covers time as a sixth-form student, initiating a railway society in hectic pre. 'A' level months, and passing on to becoming a Fine Art student at Art College. Thus photographic excursions, usually by bike, became increasingly influenced by my particular interest in the roman-ic' (impressionist, surrealist, symbolist and so on) view.

Painters such as Stanley Spencer, John Piper, Paul Nash and Laurence Lowry were influential, whilst photographers who impressed included Bill Brandt, Bert Hardy and Henri Cartier-Bresson, as well as work in the (then new) Sunday Times colour

A typical Southern Scene - flyover junction, third rail, and thundering Pacific. Hampton Court Junction April 1967.

supplements. Several railway photographers' work lingers in my memory but I quote two in particular, George Heiron and Ben Ashworth.. Then in 1964, Colin Gifford published 'Decline of Steam' - a thrilling vision of what railway photography was all about.

The appearance of this volume coincided with my photographic 'armoury' being improved by inspiring cameras: a 35mm single lens reflex - an Exakta Varex IIa and an ageing 2¼ SLR. This latter was a £25 opportunity with 80mm Tessar and 250mm Telemegor lenses.

These devices, combined with advances in film emulsions and film developers, aided my effort to record views of a means of public transport in what I can only describe as a state of annihilation. The scope for pictures was immense (1600 ASA possible!), and polite requests and evident enthusiasm opened doors and facilitated 'seized moments'. I do hope that the sense of excitement in the scenes I encountered is transmitted - other than by camera shake!

A passing thought on the topic of available (and affordable) technology combined with visual awareness: there were so many shots I missed due to factors such as manual winding, and poor focussing. Somehow though, these actions sometimes 'conjured up' more opportunities for subject matter, summed up by the phrase "one sees, rather than looks."

In retrospect, my actions remind me of an H G Wells short story (compare "The Secret Garden", and the French book "Le Grand Meaulnes") which reflects upon the idea of a once briefly glimpsed paradise, and thereafter forever searched for, without success. Ah - stolen lunch breaks on Gloucester Eastgate in June, aged eleven, enjoying a pennyworth of yesterday's cakes from the local baker…

Finally, thanks to everyone encountered in those distant days in the railway scene, and to my parents' encouragement in my wanderings when I could (or should) have been engaged in more remunerative activities….also Diana - not forgetting also the "Flying Banana", my ageing BSA, and Kevin, for railroading me into this! Similarly I feel I would regret not mentioning my indebtedness to Pete Yarlett, who introduced me to the mystery and magic of photo-processing.

Roderick Hoyle - 2007

Andover 1962 – "Daisy Dell" Bridge – A name conjuring a romantic rural retreat and until the latter part of the 20th century, it was! The steel footbridge crosses the West of England main line at the foot of 'Enham Bank', a climb to the east at 1 in 17 (see the distant plume of exhaust of a train, right of picture). Bulleid Pacific 'Winston Churchill' rolls down westbound into a frame of afternoon shadow patterns. Note well the tidy lineside, no unruly vegetation or neglected tree growth.

Left Selham 1965. This old LBSC station near Petworth suddenly appeared in spring sunlight, with all the simple but dignified charm that all small Victorian stations possessed – despite its obvious decay! The view through the filigree of branches emphasizes its elegant proportions.

Right Andover Junction – looking East 1962 – A fascinating panoramic view (typical of most station layouts throughout Britain). Cattle and horse dock to the right (note the signalman's 'Ariel' motorcycle), the busy goods shed, the four-track 'through' lines, the island platform, the left side of which accommodated the recently abandoned "Tiddley-Dyke" trains (the MSWJR's nickname) – also "Sprat & Winkle" services down the Anton & Test Valleys. To the left of the picture, the chimney of Andover 'B' signal box obscures the entrance to Andover loco shed.

Above Andover Down Sidings 1962 – The crew of the now-preserved S15 30506 awaits a clear road, slightly self-consciously! Whilst in the up sidings beyond the bridge, a Maunsell S15 simmers. The signal gantry! Semaphore signals meant that the observer could recognise anticipated trains from either front or back views. The taller right-hand one was for MSWJR traffic, a route that enabled excursions to Marlborough, Swindon, Cheltenham or even day trips to Birmingham!

Opposite Andover 1962 – Lineside "furniture" provides 'props' to complement pictorially the passing train, though taking advantage sometimes meant harmless trespass, the evident camera was self-explanatory. However, on this occasion, a nervous resident of the adjacent housing was distressed by my presence so close to the point levers - explanation was required! A yellow filter emphasises the sky and the rather carbon-rich exhaust of the 6 pm milk 'empties'.

Cranleigh 1965 – Those enthusiasts familiar with Alresford, either in BR days or as of late in preservation would relish Cranleigh for atmosphere. My occasional commute between Winchester and Surrey at weekends suggested many possible routes and in March 1965 I discovered the soon-to-be-axed ex-LBSCR branch from Guildford to Horsham (still steam!). Four months provided some solace, and Cranleigh provided much human interest- to coin a phrase for such amenable people that railman are.

The Cranleigh Signalman – sadly I never requested names - watches the Guildford train accelerate into the twilight, the briar pipe echoing less dramatically. The departing sunlight twinkles through the empty space in the single line staff instrument.

Guildford 1965 – Major earthworks resolved the space for the station and "shed" at Guildford. Occupants of the shed are silhouetted against the chalkface, whilst the remnant of the LBSCR "Interloper" in LSWR territory accelerates toward the black tunnel mouth.

Left Guildford 1965 – The contrast between the relative complexity of manoeuvres of electric units and steam was demonstrated by the Horsham service. Uncoupling, disconnection of brake and steam heating pipes and changing of indicator discs as headcode all contributed to 'atmosphere'. The fascination was doubtless less intense for the train crews is more than likely, however!

Right Andover 1962 – A scene stimulated by my art studies – I convinced myself that such scenes give more information than a sketch book, but this is the first time in 45 years that I have printed this negative! An up stopper from Salisbury accelerates away from Junction station and begins the climb to Hurstbourne past Shepherd Spring Meadows in the picture frame of an aged willow.

Alresford 1965 – Another long awaited 'discovery' thanks to scooter transport. So living in Winchester 1964-1965, a bike enabled me to take many studies of life on the charming station. Human interest was somewhat scarce at this late hour, the booking clerk's window was empty, however, the glow from the Sugg gas lamp gives enough light on this June night.

Guildford 1965 – A new venue for myself since moving to Surrey. The long focus lens 'pulls' the interesting part of the view to attention and I waited for the contrasting electric unit to appear from the tunnel.

Peasmarsh Junction north of Godalming 1965 – single line key token rituals at signalboxes command attention by observers and crews alike. Here, the foreshortening of the 250mm lens on my Meister Korelle emphasises the activity without interfering with procedures.

NO EXIT

WAITING ROOM

LADIES ROOM

REFRESHMENTS

Guildford 1965 – The anticipation of the disappearance of a typical branch train from daily life stimulated this particular view, the human interest here captured enlivens the scene. However, the scene shows how much more was to change, no ticket collector, no robust enamel signage, no phone box, the British motor bike, the once ubiquitous duffel-bag and the very tidy platform, dare I say!

Above Shawford 1965 – Not steam, but the Hampshire DEMUS were built in the traditional style – "self-service" doors, windows to poke one's head out of, comfortable seats!!!
Children being children, whilst train-spotting. Another long focus shot which balances the relative sizes of the train and the people.

Right Winchester City 1965 – A hazy January morning on Winchester's up platform, with its remarkable clock. Note the luggage barrows for the regular use of parcel traffic on passenger trains, useful also as temporary seating.

Above Southampton Docks 1962 – The wartime supplies class "USA" dock shunters were familiar workhorses up to the early sixties. Here, a visual balance has been attempted with the two machines (and note the precarious cradle for the ship's painters!!).

Opposite Winchester ex-DNS sidings at Bar End 1964 – A right-of-way caused the railway to construct an overline pedestrian bridge spanning the tracks at this goods yard on the East side of Winchester. Twice weekly, shunting operations were carried out, culminating in a small freight train departing around 1 p.m. for Eastleigh. Deft use of the shunter's pole to uncouple wagons, usually on the move, combined with timely changing of points, made fascinating spectator sport.

Above Northam Junction, Southampton 1965 – The Whitsun weekend's weather prompted a photographic excursion, always the thought "we'll not pass this way again" – to Bournemouth (from Winchester). Hanging out of the window at Northam gave the chance to catch this scene, what luck. Train crew, signalmen and exhaust – pulled together with the 250mm lens.

Opposite Waterloo 1964 – Returning to Andover one summer's evening, there was sufficient time to inspect motive power. The Salisbury crew were very co-operative with my attempts at a viewpoint but the evening sunlight emphasises the positive/negative tones 'in opposition' of the driver and fireman.

Wimbledon 1965 – An arm raised to flourish not a racquet but a green flag in response to the word "off". Note the perspective of door hinges, the scalloped shadow of LBSC valancing.

Winchester Junction 1965 – The Alton driver of the 1950's "Hampshire " unit 'lassoes' the tablet for the right of way to Alresford.

Above Winchester 1965 – The flat lighting of an evening sun from the goods yard direction enabled me to frame the 10 or 11 year old 'Standard 5' , completed by the grubby exhaust. The crew in the cab pose sympathetically!

Left Bournemouth 1965 – There is sufficient chill in the air in late May for backlit exhaust steam to swirl around Bournemouth Central. A shot highlighting the interesting 'scissors' pointwork enabling change of locos for forwarding to Weymouth.

Left
Bournemouth
1965 – The Pines
Express – but not
Bournemouth
West, alas: the
boarding
passengers
suggest few other
towns in England.

THE   PINES   E

Right Bournemouth 1965 – A fireman begins the task of preparing his "steed" for the road: Bournemouth shed from the western end of platform one.

Opposite Winchester Junction 1965 – A holiday express rushes down the 1 in 250 gradient towards Winchester and the South Coast – even 1st class is busy.

Guildford 1965 – Guildford Station takes on a Middle Eastern appearance with the arcades of roof supports. The steam shed is still fully occupied, whilst the signalman watches the Horsham branch train depart. A problem with the valve gear of the Ivatt tank causes a D65xx diesel to haul one of the last services.

Waterloo 1966 –
Waterloo's stunning glazed
roof, beautifully translucent
even in 1966 frames a
symmetrical grouping
of '2-BIL's', figures and
postal trolleys.

Above Slinfold 1965 – The Horsham Branch crosses into Sussex near Slinfold – this view of the departing train is engulfed by lush rural vegetation typifying the county.

Opposite Blandford Forum 1965 – too late I came to know Blandford in April 1965 – an idyllic photogenic station. Here in May I returned for a photo session with the Meister Korelle. The last May that a working 'Somerset & Dorset' would experience.

Andover 1962 – My Paxina 29 rollfilm camera was none-too-critical in sharpness at apertures larger than f6.3, nonetheless, this shot of S15 30823 from Mylen Bridge shunting was so 'of its time'.

Andover Junction 1962 –
A lowering evening sun on
'simmering' 'U' class Mogul
in the down sidings at
Andover gives the machine
some gravitas.

Opposite Eastleigh 1963 – A sketching trip from Art School with Graphics Tutor Kenny New (his house was named 'Gresley'!) gave us the chance to clamber over condemned locos, providing interesting viewpoints of a clutch of M7's.

Andover 1962. Why not relate the steam loco 'motif' with other machines in the landscape? This was the idea of this shot: my treasured BSA bike, and the chunky class Q1 shunting.

Hailsham 1966.
The progressive
disappearance of
rural branch lines
caused me to think
of views of lives
'lived' in rail travel,
and to try to
capture the
'environment' of
rural railways
(buildings,
carriages, lineside
fences etc). Here, a
young couple and
child struggle with
an everyday
situation at
Hailsham station,
glimpsed from the
booking hall.

Peasmarsh Junction 1965. A long shot from the A247: a Guildford train waits to gain access to the main Portsmouth line, the plume of excess steam silhouetted against the woodland.

Andover Junction 1962. It's around 1pm on a September Saturday. The Salisbury stopper struggles on the up-grade start, whilst on Platform 3, the Waterloo service is anticipated: in years past, Platform 4 would have anticipated the through Cheltenham-Southampton. (There was a route oozing with atmosphere!)

Right Andover 1962. A March evening by Gallagher's Crossing: late sun backlights an up stopper from Salisbury drifting down the grade.

Below Andover 1962. Spotters on a summer Saturday enjoy the 90 mph 'Atlantic Coast Express' passing: one of those everyday sights of simple fascination – a Wordsworth's 'Daffodils' moment. Note Andover's last working gas lamp.

Above Alresford 1964. I regret not having discovered Alresford before 'Hampshire' units took over the steeply graded Alton line. On this first visit, the 'Sugg' gas lamp caught my eye in the summer sun.

Left Hailsham branch 1965. The appropriately named Summer Hill Crossing on the truncated 'Cuckoo Line', between Polegate and Hailsham: a view that doesn't need a passing train.

Blandford 1965. Standard tank on a local service waits for the southbound through train to clear.
But why the Bournemouth line headcode here?

The contrary gradients for westbound trains out of Andover gave splendid exhaust effects on winter's days – and here sunlight creates sparkle. Beyond, the gantry signals an up 'stopper', and the variety of wagon shapes in the up sidings: note also the pattern of the trackwork.

Eastleigh 1963. Winchester's B4 station pilot / shunter spent its weekends at Eastleigh, though I never witnessed its transit. This picture provided the basis for a wood engraving - so many textures.

Another 35mm shot from a sequence as 'illumination' was prepared for this 1846 built station on the Bishopstoke to Salisbury Milford route. The booking clerk / porter / station master begins the daily routine of Tilley lamps as daylight wanes one September day.

Above Spetisbury, near Blandford 1965. Late April – leafless trees: no climate change then! Spetisbury Church and the Stour Valley frame this Blandford bound S & D train - , caught during a short camping trip to Dorset.

Left North of Winchester 1964. One of the interloping 35mm shots in this collection: where, pictorially, fate assisted my intentions. Two foreigners slowly making their way to Eastleigh on the LSW main line needed a background: lo and behold the farmer appeared, bow saw over his arm, at the appropriate moment – and the Ford Consul was not hidden by his trilby as he walked! A technical post-script: this was one of my first excursions using a new Zeiss Flektogon 35/2.8. The standard 50mm Tessar was too restricted in its field of view.

Andover 1962. Another sample of the winter light on departing 'stoppers' from start – accompanied by an up train rolling into Platform 3. The rising gradient - about 1 in 300 - was enough to produce some pleasing exhaust effects.

Salisbury 1964. Preparation for the Waterloo run at the east end: mailbags in the foreground, numerous railwaymen, soft August sunlight. This visit was motivated by an impending move from this area.

Andover 1962. A view of Andover motivated by a wish to use evening light and 'active' exhaust though not on up trains - a mixture of Maunsell and Bulleid carriages with a 1950s loco are backed by the flour mill of MacDougall's.

Exeter 1961. A week-long 'West of England Rail-Rover' gave me an opportunity to visit many doomed branches in August 1961 – but maximum use of travel limited photographs of any great merit. However, one could hang out of the window, and here a Maunsell Mogul – we missed the Drummond T9s – clambers up the 1 in 40 between St David's and Central stations.

Above Baynards 1965. May time in Sussex – a photographer readies his equipment to catch an Ivatt 2-6-2T departing for Horsham. Baynards signalman was an enthusiastic dahlia grower on the station platforms – the show was just beginning in June as closure descended.

Right Grateley 1962. Salisbury Plain as a railway venue is difficult pictorially, but I'm happy with this March viewpoint: the headcode gives a sharp focal point, despite the eye-catching telegraph pole.

Steventon 1965. Capturing a viewpoint which exploits the facility of the camera to catch a passing moment can help make an unpromising viewpoint 'live'. Here, the aim is to be a passing motorist or pedestrian at a point when suddenly a train passes.

Another view of Shepherd's Spring Meadows. Here the rebuilt 'West Country' is making a determined attack on the facing gradient: the cool spring air holds the exhaust beautifully.

Andover 1964. Non-stop expresses through Andover demanded a different treatment to 'Express' their haste. I was familiar with the Italian Futurists' paintings of arrested action: 'panning' the camera would freeze the static and blur the active, or ancillary areas. Not to everyone's taste, but the crew and the trainspotters add to the depth.

Winchester 1964. Another 'glimpse' shot, though anticipated: the passing 'Bournemouth Belle', waiting passengers and the patterns of out of focus valencing.

Above Andover 1962. A varied freight arrives from the truncated MSWJR, the crew having just returned the single line key to the signalman at 'B' box.

Left Walton on Thames 1966. An occasion when a picture has been created from unpromising material – tall mesh fence bordering a dull cutting. I chose to keep the cycle as foreground, and the train panned would dissipate the mesh fence. Luckily, the fireman was visible, and an interesting exhaust accelerating from a signal slack.

Salisbury 1964. Another quiet study of the Salisbury driver oiling on 'Merchant Navy' 35007. Salisbury locos were always in fine fettle in these latter days.

Alresford 1964. The first day of summertime in March 1964 – the signalman on duty converses with the Alton train Guard, whilst a couple – as in my study of Hailsham Station – manipulate a folding push-chair.

Alresford 1964. Having found an elevated viewpoint with my 250mm lens, I took a sequence of arrival and departure shots of a Sunday train. This view sums up the atmosphere of a cherished branch line station – now happily preserved.

Above Andover 1964. A fellow photographer helps to 'arrest' the movement out of the picture – pictorially! – of one of the extra Summer Saturday 'ACE's'. I vaguely recall his camera was a 'bullseye' Zeiss Contarex – a camera built like a steam train!

Left Ash 1964. This grouping of lamps, barrows and decorative valancing, needed a passing train to obliterate a 'busy' background: a Mogul obliged after a wait, emphasizing the backlighting.

Above Winchester 1965. February brought an inviting several inches of snow to Winchester: here the 'Bournemouth Belle' rushes down the 1 in 250 with a slight blurring of the smokebox.

Left Ropley 1965. Turning off the A31 at the east end of the village taking the lane to Bighton, I glimpsed this view of the station: a train duly arrived, but the only indication of life was the guard giving the 'right-away' – a moment to release the shutter.

Left Blandford 1965. Arriving at Blandford Station for the first time one April evening:, the pictorial possibilities made my day – here is one where the light and the 'action' happened as anticipated.

Right Bournemouth Central 1965. I was reminded of the classic Southern Railway poster at a platform end, though in this case the child is somewhat older.

Lower right Wareham 1965. Not a very stimulating station at platform level, but I have tried to use the 'clutter' to make a frame.

10

BOURNEMOUTH BELLE
First and Second Class · Pullman Cars Only

TO ENSURE THE
PUNCTUAL
DEPARTURE OF
TRAIN, THIS
BARRIER WILL
BE CLOSED
IMMEDIATELY
BEFORE THE
TRAIN IS DUE TO
DEPART

PLEASE
SHOW
TICKETS

Left Waterloo 1966. A 'grab it while it's there' shot' – and happily not all the passengers had their backs to my lens. Would such orderly behaviour be present at Waterloo in 2007?

Above Bournemouth West 1965. How to reflect the impending end of this pleasant station, due that autumn? This opportunity suddenly occurred: the railman looked like an undertaker, a slower shutter speed blurred the departing empty stock, the rubbish bin was appropriate and the window framed the view.

Above Bournemouth west 1965. Another memory at this station – though a crew in the cab would complete the picture.

Right Wareham 1965. I forgot how long a wait it was before a figure came by to give scale and interest!

LOAD 2 TONS DISTRIBUTED

Left Worgret, near Wareham 1965. This junction gave several interesting views of main and branch line trains, and the view of the box is enlivened by the Standard '5' restarting from a check.

Lower left Templecombe 1965. I took a last through trip in January from Bristol to Bournemouth, and caught this view on the return trip. A lamp post provided stability for the camera, with the signalman busy at his register.

Right Swanage 1965. A springtime arrival at the terminus – the semaphore signals graphically frame the handover of the single line token.

Templecombe 1965. This was a glorious place of industrial Railwayana in the midst of rural Somerset: the manual turntable, and endless supply of brake shoes (reflecting the wear and tear of these on the descents in the Mendips.)

Clapham Junction 1966. Photographers frame the view of a Weymouth express – I regret not taking another shot as they turned to follow the train, to identify their cameras.

Above Feltham 1966. A long exposure in dismal weather disembodies a passing figure at this rather bleak shed.

Left Feltham 1966. An abandoned S15 in the remnants of this once important marshalling yard: excessive supplies of water!

Above Andover 1962: Vigo Road, Picket Piece crossroads. This view of a down express has much topographical significance: 'progress' has annihilated the rurality of this view. The lane here shown is now the route through a large industrial estate, covering the fields up to the railway. Anticipation of this fate prompted the less than perfect shot.

Opposite top Andover – West, 1961. Days after 'A' levels gave time to explore viewpoints around Andover: here, west of the village of Monxton, a panoramic view of a typical stopping train from Salisbury. Here is a Maunsell 'S15', a utility van, and a 5-set Bulleid coaching stock beyond the waving barley.

Opposite lower Andover 1962. The down Atlantic Coast Express rushes Platform 2 at over 90 mph. To the extreme left a Maunsell mogul simmers on the site of the ex MSWJ shed.

Above Micheldever 1962. The train and the clothing evoke a different 'country' - as L P Hartley would have said.

Right Andover 1962. Evening light on Andover's 'B' box and an accelerating Merchant Navy approaching Mylen Road bridge.

Above Esher 1966. Crossing the River Mole, the nameless Pacific has a year of active service remaining.

Left Andover 1962. West of Andover an up express complements the receding perspective of telegraph wires, rails, and fence posts. (What a tidy vista!)

Left Guildford 1966. An October day emphasizes the exhaust steam with serious matters under discussion.

Right Bath S&D Shed 1966. Subject matter such as this was so attractive – but so inefficient in operation.

Peasmarsh 1966. The box, having been closed for a year, needed a different approach. This view was a gift: the lines of the foreground lead one's eye to the subject, with a blurring of the passing electric unit.

Right Winchester 1963. An afternoon commuter train chatters past St Cross allotments south of Winchester: the waiting was worth it, with the gardener in perfect 'pose'.

Lower Guildford 1966. Silhouettes are always appealing – and the two figures of lamp-man and the guard just happened to be simultaneously correct in visual terms.

Walton-on-Thames 1967. A hazardous viewpoint in suburban Surrey – with only my ears to detect a train – the 'Bournemouth Belle'. What a show of British vehicles – and vintage shop fronts! How we were amused at the Heinz beans poster…

Left Andover 1962. A prolonged stop at Andover junction for unloading parcels and topping up water supplies gives a 'busy' photograph. (I should have taken more.)

Right Poole 1965. The Somerset and Dorset had a short reprieve beyond the original axing of late 1965 – as a student '65-'66 in Bristol, I was therefore able to take one last return trip in January. Here, at Poole 'en route' sunlight prevails towards journey's end. Lively passengers and watchful driver fill the frame of the 250mm lens from the carriage window,

Left Bournemouth 1966. Father and son soak up the atmosphere of a steam shed in its last months – the 250mm lens confined the scale of the group.

Lower left Eastleigh 1963. Though most schoolboys were not so splendidly uniformed, his presence typifies a mid 20th century trainspotter amongst these antique giants.

Right Eastleigh 1963. Another view from a cab roof - an M7 this time contrasting "the quick and the dead". In the foreground a recently retired 'B4' shunter, awaiting its fate.

Micheldever 1962
This 1840 station was an energetic cycle ride from home in Andover, along a docile A303, and past the recently demolished Longparish branch overbridge. The March sunlight on 'Lord Nelson' catches the attention of a trainspotting sparrow. Yes it is 30850, now back in service - bravo!